Hallucinogens
Unreal Visions

ILLICIT AND MISUSED DRUGS

ILLICIT AND MISUSED DRUGS

Hallucinogens
Unreal Visions

by Sheila Nelson

Mason Crest Publishers
Philadelphia

Mason Crest Publishers Inc.
370 Reed Road
Broomall, Pennsylvania 19008
(866) MCP-BOOK (toll free)
www.masoncrest.com

15 14 13 12 11 10   9 8 7 6 5 4 3 2

Library of Congress Cataloging-in-Publication Data
ISBN-13: 978-1-4222-0149-7 (series)

Nelson, Sheila.
  Hallucinogens : unreal visions / by Sheila Nelson.
     p. cm. — (Illicit and misused drugs)
  Includes bibliographical references and index.
  ISBN 978-1-4222-0155-8
  1. Hallucinogenic drugs—Juvenile literature. 2. Hallucinogenic
plants—Juvenile literature. 3. Drug abuse. I. Title.
HV5822.H25N45 2008
613.8'3—dc22
                                        2007010789

Interior design by Benjamin Stewart.
Cover design by MK Bassett-Harvey.
Produced by Harding House Publishing Service Inc.
Vestal, New York.
www.hardinghousepages.com

Cover image design by Peter Spires Culotta.
Cover photography: iStock Photography (Spectral-Design,
     Piotr Wielopolski)
Printed in the Hashemite Kingdom of Jordan.

CONTENTS

INTRODUCTION

Addicting drugs are among the greatest challenges to health, well-being, and the sense of independence and freedom for which we all strive—and yet these drugs are present in the everyday lives of most people. Almost every home has alcohol or tobacco waiting to be used, and has medicine cabinets stocked with possibly outdated but still potentially deadly drugs. Almost everyone has a friend or loved one with an addiction-related problem. Almost everyone seems to have a solution neatly summarized by word or phrase: medicalization, legalization, criminalization, war-on-drugs.

For better and for worse, drug information seems to be everywhere, but what information sources can you trust? How do you separate misinformation (whether deliberate or born of ignorance and prejudice) from the facts? Are prescription drugs safer than "street" drugs? Is occasional drug use really harmful? Is cigarette smoking more addictive than heroin? Is marijuana safer than alcohol? Are the harms caused by drug use limited to the users? Can some people become addicted following just a few exposures? Is treatment or counseling just for those with serious addiction problems?

These are just a few of the many questions addressed in this series. It is an empowering series because it provides the information and perspectives that can help people come to their own opinions and find answers to the challenges posed by drugs in their own lives. The series also provides further resources for information and assistance, recognizing that no single source has all the answers. It should be of interest and relevance to areas of study spanning biology, chemistry, history, health, social studies and more. Its efforts to provide a real-world context for the information that is clearly presented but not overly simplified should be appreciated by students, teachers, and parents.

The series is especially commendable in that it does not pretend to pose easy answers or imply that all decisions can be made on the basis of simple facts: some challenges have no immediate or simple solutions, and some solutions will need to rely as much upon basic values as basic facts. Despite this, the series should help to at least provide a foundation of knowledge. In the end, it may help as much by pointing out where the solutions are not simple, obvious, or known to work. In fact, at many points, the reader is challenged to think for him- or herself by being asked what his or her opinion is.

A core concept of the series is to recognize that we will never have all the facts, and many of the decisions will never be easy. Hopefully, however, armed with information, perspective, and resources, readers will be better prepared for taking on the challenges posed by addictive drugs in everyday life.

—*Jack E. Henningfield, Ph.D.*

1 What Are Hallucinogens?

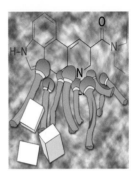

It started out awesome, then it became scary. I was with my best friends and one of them looked really weird to me. Her tongue was like a snake's and her head started to spin around. I freaked!!! I had to go into another room with other people tripping. . . . Another friend turned into the devil and I looked in the mirror and turned into a demon. My heart started to beat really fast and I thought I was going to die. I finally got over my fear of my best friend and went into the room with them again. They were watching *Wizard of Oz* and everything was just unreal. I'm so happy I survived. I wanted the trip to end really bad when I saw the devil. I kept thinking I was going to die. I had to have my best friend's brother keep on telling me I was going to be fine and when I woke up everyone will be okay. I'll probably end up doing it again but I hope it's a lot better next time. (On-line first-person account from http://paranoia.lycaeum.org/stories/lsd)

Seeing things that aren't really there, thinking thoughts you would never normally have thought: hallucinogenic drugs work on the body by altering the way a person thinks, feels, or experiences reality. Some of these drugs are found in nature, while others are created in laboratories. While

Hallucinogenic drugs make users see things that aren't really there and think thoughts they would never normally experience.

all these drugs affect the chemicals in the brain, they do not all work in the same way. The effects of each drug are slightly different, even though they all change perceptions.

The brain is a very complex organ that is not yet fully understood. Because of this, scientists do not know exactly how most hallucinogens affect the brain. Recent advances in science, however, have helped them determine that LSD, for example, affects one type of serotonin receptor. Serotonin is a neurotransmitter, a chemical used to carry messages throughout the brain and body. While many drugs, both legal and illegal, affect serotonin, not all of them cause hallucinations. Only when the brain's delicate chemistry is shifted in a certain way do hallucinations occur.

LSD

In 1938, a Swiss doctor named Albert Hofmann worked for a pharmaceutical company called Sandoz. His job was to experiment with medicinal plants and create medicines from their chemicals. He started working with ergot, a fungus that grows mainly on rye, combining lysergic acid—the active chemical in ergot—with a variety of chemicals known as amines. Hofmann found that one of these lysergic acid compounds created a drug that could be used to stop bleeding after childbirth; he continued his research with interest.

Hofmann's twenty-fifth lysergic acid compound was LSD, lysergic acid combined with diethylamide. (LSD stands for the German *Lyserg-säure-diäthylamid*, meaning lysergic acid diethylamide.) LSD did not seem to have any dramatic medical effects, although it did make the laboratory animals restless.

A person taking LSD may "see" music or "hear" colors; flowers may have faces; and time may seem to move differently.

For five years, Hofmann worked on other projects, thinking little about LSD, until in 1943 he began to experiment with it again. One day, while working with the chemical, he spilled a little on his bare hand. He started feeling dizzy and on edge and went home to lie down. He lay on his bed with his eyes closed, feeling very odd. Pictures, colors, and shapes danced and sparkled on the inside of his eyelids. After about two hours, the strange sensations began to disappear.

At first, Hofmann did not realize what had caused his experience. When he remembered spilling the chemical on his hand, he decided to take a larger dose on purpose and write down what he experienced. He took a dose of 250 micrograms of LSD and asked his assistant to stay with him and see how the chemical affected him. He

Albert Hofmann is considered to be the Father of LSD.

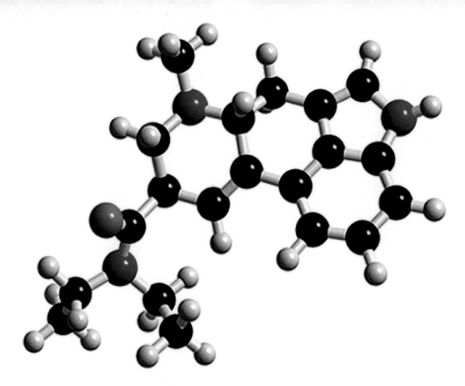

A portrayal of LSD as a chemical molecule.

believed this would be a small and safe amount with which to start self-experimenting. (In fact, LSD is such a powerful drug that this was a very large dose.) For the next several hours, Hofmann experienced terrifying hallucinations and bizarre emotions. The face of the woman next door turned evil and monstrous. The room danced and twisted around him. He thought he must be dying—or going insane. He gulped milk, hoping this would stop the reaction. When the drug finally began to wear off, Hofmann was exhausted, but he had begun to actually enjoy the strange sensations.

This was the first of many self-experiments Hofmann made with LSD. His colleagues, too, took the drug to experience the effects for themselves. They believed that such a powerful substance must have medical uses. The effects of LSD led them to conclude that it might be

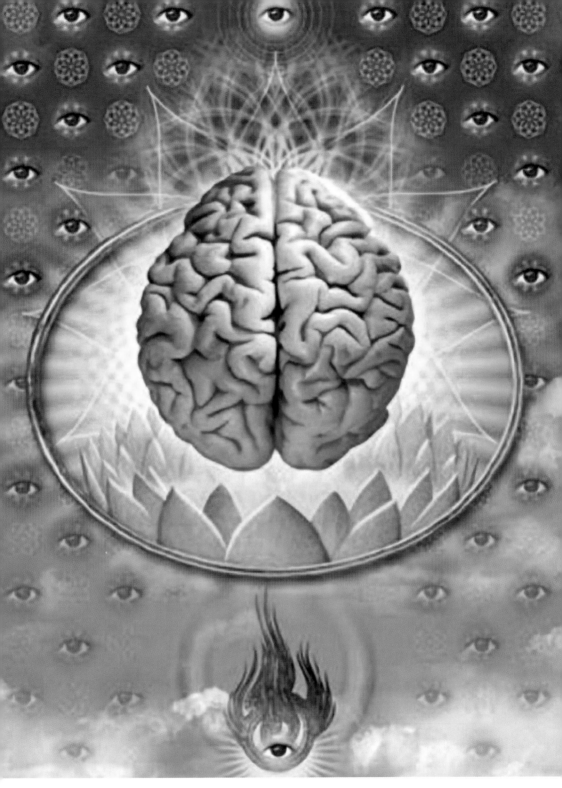

LSD alters the way one perceives the world.

useful in treating mental illnesses such as *schizophrenia* or conditions such as alcoholism.

The next step in developing LSD as an accepted medication was human trials. During the 1950s, researchers from pharmaceutical companies and universities in various parts of the world conducted many studies to explore the effects of LSD and its possible uses as a treatment. Prisoners were given the drug to see whether it might change any criminal tendencies they might have; besides, prisoners were sometimes considered free test subjects in those days. People with schizophrenia and other psychiatric conditions received LSD to test whether it could be a useful treatment option with fewer side effects than many of the options at the time. Alcoholics were studied to see if LSD might help them stop drinking. Many scientists were excited about the possibility that LSD could be a new miracle drug.

After ten years of experimentation, though, most researchers reluctantly admitted that LSD would never be a reliable treatment. Despite the fact that thousands of articles had been published declaring LSD was useful, successful, and a great contribution to modern medicine, the truth was that LSD had far too many problems to be really useful. For one thing, the effects were not consistent. Two people could be given the same dose and have two completely different reactions. Some people had calm experiences that left them feeling peaceful and enlightened. Others saw terrifying visions and felt bewildering sensations. Some were so affected by LSD that they never recovered, dying by suicide or living the rest of their lives in an institution.

Even though most of the scientists and pharmaceutical companies had dismissed LSD as a useful drug, some

In the 1950s, scientists were hopeful that they would find a way to use LSD as a treatment for schizophrenia.

Timothy Leary was a Harvard professor who encouraged students to use LSD to "expand their minds."

researchers and university students began taking it just for the experience. In the early years of the 1960s, before LSD became illegal in 1967, thousands of people tried LSD. They were encouraged by people like Timothy Leary and Richard Alpert, Harvard psychology professors who believed LSD could keep criminals from committing more crimes and alcoholics from drinking and could give deep spiritual insights. After the drug was banned, chemists in illegal laboratories synthesized LSD to sell to users.

LSD is almost always ingested—taken by mouth—most commonly using blotter paper. When LSD is made, it is in crystal form. It is then dissolved in liquid and this liquid usually soaked up by a piece of blotter paper. The blotter paper often has patterns or psychedelic designs printed on it. The paper is then dried and cut into tiny squares, with each square being one dose. Users take the drug by putting the square on their tongue and letting it dissolve. Sometimes, the liquid is mixed with gelatin and made into thin sheets called "windowpane." Other ways

LSD has been taken include: soaked into a sugar cube, in tiny tablets, or even mixed into eye drops. In the 1960s, when LSD use was most widespread, a typical dose was 100 to 200 micrograms. Today, a dose is usually only 20 to 100 micrograms. This is because the drug is so powerful that only a very small amount can create an intense experience. LSD usually takes effect within thirty minutes of ingesting it, and the effects can last for twelve hours or even longer.

Generally, the effects of a dose of LSD can be felt with half an hour of ingesting it. Physical changes come first, often causing dizziness, increased heart rate, or nausea. Within an hour, a person can begin to feel a sense of unreality and the beginnings of visual hallucinations, such as colors and lights. Time is often experienced differently while under the influence of LSD, so that a few seconds might feel like an hour. The effects usually peak about one to two hours after taking LSD and have worn off after four to twelve hours. The experience of taking LSD or other hallucinogens is frequently called a trip, and a bad experience is called a bad trip. A person is often tired after the drug wears off and can have a headache. For some people, LSD can take a very long time to wear off, up to twenty-four hours at times. The effects of LSD vary a great deal and depend on the dose, a person's emotions, the setting where a person takes the drugs, and whether or not any other drugs have been taken at the same time.

After only a few days of taking LSD, the body builds up a tolerance. This means that a person does not experience as strong a high from the drug with the same dosage. In addition, people who have developed a tolerance for LSD also show an increased tolerance for certain other hallucinogens, such as psilocybin and mescaline. Tolerance

Harvard professor Richard Alpert believed that LSD use yielded deep spiritual insights.

LSD is usually ingested from blotter paper, which is often printed with designs (such as those shown here).

Ecstasy

Ecstasy, the most common name for MDMA (methylenedioxymethamphet-amine), is a difficult drug to classify. It is usually known as a club drug, since it is popular in clubs and at parties. Sometimes called an emphathogen because it can produce feelings of empathy in users, ecstasy acts as a stimulant, but can have hallucinogenic effects at high doses. Ecstasy has been known to lead to serious medical emergencies or death, for example, from kidney failure caused by a very high body temperature.

is experienced with many drugs after prolonged usage and addicts of drugs such as cocaine and heroine tend to cope by taking larger amounts to get the same high. These drugs are addictive, however, and LSD is not. While LSD users may continue taking the drug because they like the high, they do not experience physical or psychological withdrawal if they do not take it. Taking larger and larger amounts to achieve the same high is not common among LSD users, since the larger the dose the more likely a person will experience a "bad trip"—with terrifying hallucinations and unpleasant physical sensations. The body's tolerance to LSD also wears off after several days. This means that the typical LSD user often takes the drug only every month or every few weeks.

PCP and Ketamine

PCP is known as a dissociative drug, meaning that is causes people to feel disconnected from their bodies and the world around them. Its full name is 1-phenyl cyclohexyl piperidine, sometimes called phencyclidine.

Like LSD, PCP was developed by a pharmaceutical company for use as a legitimate drug. It was created in

Ecstasy is ingested in the form of colorful tablets.

1926 and thirty years later, in 1956, Dr. Vincent Maddox and Dr. Graham Chen, working for the Parke Davis pharmaceutical company in Detroit, Michigan, began experimenting with it. Maddox and Chen discovered that PCP could act as an **opiate**, a **stimulant**, a **sedative**, and a hallucinogen, which is unusual, since most drugs act as only one of these types. Users were affected differently depending on the size of the dose and the person's **metabolism**. They could be wildly excited and energized, or they could be left in a **catatonic** state for hours. Parke Davis began to develop the drug for use as an anesthetic called Sernyl, meaning serenity. Tests showed that PCP caused unconsciousness and lack of pain so that patients could be operated on, and, even better, PCP did not seem to have the dangers of the anesthetics being used at that time. While a double dose of most anesthetics would be fatal because breathing and heart rate was slowed so dramatically, it took twenty-six times a regular dose of PCP to kill a person. Unfortunately, patients who had taken PCP often woke up from their surgeries agitated and hallucinating. Because of this, Parke Davis stopped testing on the drug, although it was used for a while longer as an anesthetic for animals.

Scientists wondered if they could change the chemicals in PCP just a little, so that it would still work as an anesthetic without the bad side effects. These experiments gave them ketamine, similar to PCP although less powerful. Today, ketamine is used in veterinary medicine and sometimes as an anesthetic for people. Because it can cause hallucinations and bizarre sensations, though, doctors use it less often than other anesthetics.

PCP and ketamine are addictive, causing regular users to crave more and more of them. However, with PCP especially, the effects can be so frightening that many people do not intentionally take the drug more than once. The combination of delusions and detachment that PCP—and to a lesser extent ketamine—causes can make people do extremely dangerous things. Users often feel like they are indestructible and cannot be hurt. People are much more likely to die from doing crazy things while taking PCP than they are from an overdose of the drug.

PCP is taken in several ways. Most often, it is sprinkled on mint, oregano, parsley, or marijuana leaves and then smoked. Sometimes it is ingested or injected or inhaled through the nose in powder form. Ketamine is taken in similar ways, although it is less commonly smoked. How these drugs are taken determines how long it takes before their effects are felt—inhaling the smoke is the quickest, with the effects felt about a minute later, while ingesting the drug brings effects after approximately half an hour. Ketamine's effects last around an hour and the effects of PCP can last eight hours or even for several days.

Peyote and Mescaline

While LSD and PCP were created in the twentieth century, some hallucinogenic drugs have been used for thousands of years. For example, peyote, a cactus that grows in the southwestern United States and Mexico, has been used in religious ceremonies by some Native American peoples throughout history.

Peyote is a small cactus without any spines. The top of the cactus is covered with "buttons," which are harvested for use as a hallucinogen. These buttons are dried and either chewed whole or ground into powder. They are sometimes brewed into a tea and, occasionally, smoked.

Peyote is a small cactus that has been used for centuries by Native American groups as part of their religious practices.

Peyote users often see swirls of color, while their perception of time is altered.

A petroglyph from Texas portrays the Huichol Indians' prehistoric peyote use.

Peyote is extremely bitter and those ingesting it often experience nausea and vomiting before they begin to experience changes in sensations.

The hallucinatory effects of peyote are similar to LSD, although the drug is much less powerful. Like LSD, a user's perception of time is altered, so that he may feel as though many hours have passed when, in reality, only a few minutes have gone by. Users often see swirls of color and images of people or animals. Physically, peyote increases blood pressure and heart rate and dilates the pupils.

The main *psychoactive* component of peyote is mescaline. Mescaline can be created in a laboratory, as crystals that are ingested for a high similar to that of peyote. The effect is not exactly the same, since peyote also contains other active compounds besides mescaline.

Peyote is one of the few drugs in the United States that is legal for a select group of people. Since some Native American groups have used peyote in their religious rites for centuries, lawmakers declared that this use was protected as a First Amendment, Freedom of Religion, right. Only members of the Native American Church have the right to use peyote and a person cannot become a member unless she is part of a federally recognized tribe. Peyote is also legal in Canada; however, mescaline is illegal in both the United States and Canada.

Psilocybin Mushrooms

Like peyote, psilocybin mushrooms have been used by native peoples in Mexico and Central America for thousands of years. Statues of mushrooms have been discovered from as long ago as 500 BCE, which archaeologists believe were used in worship ceremonies. Psilocybin mushrooms contain a psychoactive compound called psilocin that creates a less powerful LSD-like effect.

Psilocybin mushrooms, often called Magic Mushrooms or shrooms, are usually dried and eaten. Sometimes, though, the psychoactive chemicals in the mushrooms are created separately and sold as a white powder.

In the United States, psilocybin mushrooms have become the second-most popular hallucinogen, after LSD. They are not the only hallucinogenic mushroom, however; most mushrooms in the same family as psilocybin also cause hallucinations, but many of these are extremely poisonous.

Psilocybin mushrooms contain a hallucinogenic chemical.

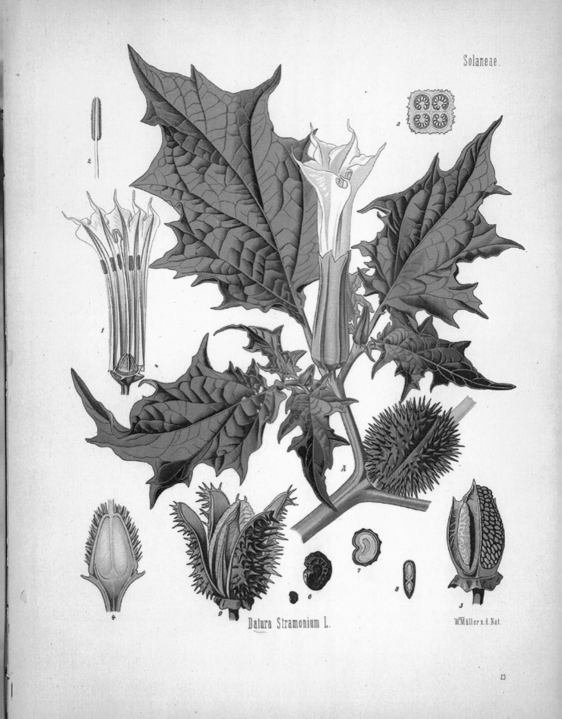

Jimson weed contains a dangerous hallucinogen that can make users very ill, or even kill them.

Jimson Weed

Jimson weed is a plant that grows wild in most parts of the world. Its real name is *Datura stramonium*, but it is also called a number of other names, such as thorn apple, devil's apple, gypsum weed, and zombie's cucumber. Jimson weed contains the belladonna alkaloids atropine and scopolamine, which are found also in plants like deadly nightshade and the mandrake root. These plants have been used throughout history as medicines, beauty treatments, and poisons.

A jimson weed flower; this plant grows wild in most parts of the world.

Jimson weed is actually one of the most dangerous hallucinogens, although it is rarely used. While it is difficult to overdose on LSD or PCP, the amount of jimsonweed needed to experience a high is not much less than the amount it takes to overdose. It is also dangerous because of the physical effects it causes. Body temperatures can rise to such extremes that brain damage can occur, and users can experience dramatically increased heart rates and difficulty breathing. People who have taken jimson weed often become totally separated from reality. They believe they are interacting with the world around them, but they are in fact experiencing vivid hallucinations. They often act bizarrely, and do not even notice sounds and sights around them. The drug also causes amnesia, so people do not remember the experience afterward. The belladonna alkaloid atropine causes the physical effects, while scopolamine causes the hallucinations and behavior changes.

The name "jimson weed" comes from "Jamestown weed," because of a famous poisoning that occurred in 1676 in the English colony in Jamestown, Virginia. The incident happened when a group of people ate salad containing the plant. After they began hallucinating and acting strangely, they were confined for several days until the effects wore off.

The unpleasant and extreme effects of jimson weed make it an unpopular drug, but it is sometimes taken by teenagers looking for a cheap high. These cases make the evening news every few years because it often makes users very sick, when it does not kill them.

Many other hallucinogens exist, both in nature and created in laboratories. Most of these are very similar to the

Jimson weed's name comes from the colony of Jamestown, where a group of people ate the plant in 1676 and began acting very strangely!

Hallucinogenic chemicals occur naturally in a variety of plants and fungi; as a result, human beings have experimented with these substances for thousands of years.

more common hallucinogenic drugs like LSD and psilo-cybin. Naturally occurring hallucinogens are usually from the same family of plants as more powerful substances, while the artificially created ones generally have only very small chemical differences from more familiar drugs.

Because hallucinogens do occur in nature, people have been aware of them for many thousands of years. The history of hallucinogenic drug use has been long and varied.

2 The History of Hallucinogens

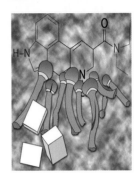

Everything in the room was changing colors. The ceiling had screaming faces swirling about. But the strangest part of the trip was the feeling inside my head. It was as if my entire thinking process was wiped out. I could barely remember my name, nothing made sense to me, it was as if my thoughts were intoxicated. My hearing seemed to be as distorted as my sight. All the sounds I heard were not distinct sounds but a blur of multiple sounds colliding with one another. . . . I have probably tripped over 30 times now, but that was my best experience in LSD. I hope to find it again someday. (On-line first-person account from http:// paranoia.lycaeum.org/stories/lsd/)

People have been using hallucinogens for centuries. From prehistoric peoples finding a connection with the gods to teenagers looking for a new kind of high, hallucinogen users have existed all over the world throughout history. While newer hallucinogens such as LSD or PCP are created in laboratories, hallucinogenic plants and fungi have been around for a very long time. Archaeologists have found ancient rock paintings in various parts of the world that seem to show people experiencing the effects of hallucinogenic mushrooms—some from as long ago as 7000 BCE. In general, this art suggests a link between the mushrooms and the religious life of the ancient peoples. Many people, both ancient and modern, have believed hallucinogenic substances allowed them to communicate with the gods and to understand deep mysteries about the universe. Often, shamans or priests have controlled the use of these substances and used them in religious ceremonies.

The ancient Hindu scriptures known as the Vedas mention a sacred drink called Soma. The drink was made from a mountain plant and was said to be what the gods drank. Today, some people believe that Soma was hallucinogenic, partly because of its use in religious ceremonies. No one knows for sure, though, what Soma really was. Information about things that happened thousands, or even hundreds, of years ago, is frequently limited and can be difficult to interpret.

In Greece, from about 1500 BCE until 392 CE, every five years priests of Demeter, the Greek goddess of grain and agriculture, led participants in a nine-day ritual called the Eleusinian Mysteries. During the ceremony, the people drank Kykeon, a mixture of water, barley, and herbs. No one knows whether kykeon really had hallucinogenic properties, but some people have speculated that the ergot fungus—from which LSD is derived—might have been grown on the barley used in the drink.

Into the Twentieth Century

Doctors and other healers have always used plants as medicines. By accident, or by trial and error, people learned which plants stopped bleeding, which eased

Not all hallucinogenic trips are pleasant. Some are bizarre or even frightening.

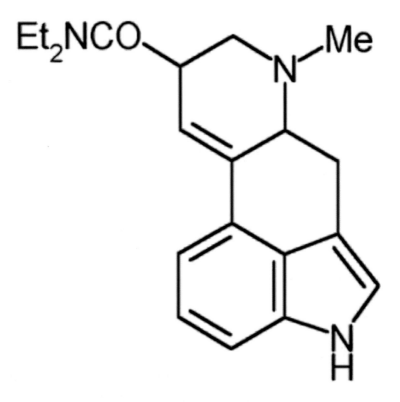

A diagram of LSD's chemical structure; as scientists learned more about chemistry, pharmaceutical companies were built based on their research.

stomach aches, which cured headache or bad breath or fever. They also learned which plants were good to eat and which were deadly poison. This knowledge was passed down from generation to generation, sometimes orally and later written on scrolls or in books. People did not know a lot about why these plants affected the body the way they did. It was not until the nineteenth and early twentieth centuries that advances in chemistry and technology allowed scientists to begin to understand the chemicals these plants contained and how these chemicals interacted with the body.

The new discoveries about chemical structures led to the founding of many pharmaceutical companies. These companies began experimenting with well-known medicinal plants, separating out the chemicals that acted as medicine and packaging them as pills or syrups. While looking for medicines in plants, pharmaceutical companies had many failures; sometimes the chemicals they isolated from the plants seemed to do nothing, and sometimes, such as with LSD, the effects were not useful. Sometimes, even though the chemical helped the body in one way, the side effects were so extreme that the drug could not be used. This was the case with PCP, which was originally created as an anesthetic. Drugs such as heroin and cocaine were also used for a time as medicines, until they were banned because of their negative effects.

When pharmaceutical companies researched the effects of LSD and other hallucinogens, they used volunteers—or prisoners or psychiatric patients—to figure out the best uses for these drugs, along with the side effects and dosages. When the trials ended in failure, some of these volunteers decided they liked the effects of the drugs they had taken. Scientists who had experimented on themselves, and university students who had been a part of LSD research, began using the drugs on their own time and sharing them with their friends. In this way, drugs like LSD jumped from the labs to the streets.

The CIA and LSD

In 1950, the United States entered the Korean War, fighting on the side of South Korea against the invasion by the communist North. After only a few months of war, the North Koreans released radio broadcasts of American prisoners of war condemning the American government and way of life and claiming they now believed communism was the right and only way to live. Americans became gripped with the fear that these men had been brainwashed, that people's minds could be changed by force, and that this could happen to anyone. In reality, very few American POWs actually converted to communism.

The CIA worried that communist countries had really figured out how to brainwash people. In fact, even before the Korean War began, the CIA had already begun working on a project to study mind control. This project, and others that followed it, used LSD—along with things like hypnotism and electroshock treatments—to experiment with mind control and social control. The CIA wanted to know if they could use LSD to control enemy agents, whether LSD would act as a truth drug and possibly a brainwashing tool. Most of those participating in the experiments were prisoners or psychiatric patients. Even though the law requires that people give informed consent to take part in medical experiments, few of these people knew they were part of an experiment or what they had been given.

Dr. Sidney Gottlieb headed the LSD testing project MKULTRA. Dr. Gottlieb recruited several doctors to run the actual experiments. One of these, Dr. Ewen Cameron, worked out of a hospital in Montreal, Canada. Dr. Gottlieb argued to the CIA that because the experiments were being done outside of the United States, they could claim that no American citizens had been harmed by the testing.

The CIA also wondered if they could use LSD on leaders or officials from other countries to affect their actions.

U.S. involvement in the Korean War played a role in the history of LSD. The CIA conducted experiments to determine if the drug could be used to brainwash enemy agents, thus possibly saving the lives of American military in combat situations.

Scientists eventually abandoned their experiments with LSD as a possible military tool, and turned their attention elsewhere.

They decided they probably would not have to brainwash the person—they could just slip some LSD into his drink and then watch as he began acting crazy. Someone on LSD who tried to speak at an important meeting, for example, would look ridiculous and would not be able to present his arguments well. A leader who had been given LSD and then appeared in public might convince his citizens he was unstable and stir up groups of his own people to try and get rid of him.

In order to see how a person might act who had secretly been given LSD in everyday life, CIA agents began slipping doses of the drug into each other's drinks or the drinks of friends. They then recorded what happened and had the drugged person write down his own experiences as well. These experiments sometimes caused bad reactions and appear to have led to the death of one man, a scientist named Frank Olson who became depressed and paranoid after having been given LSD; several weeks later, he crashed to his death from a tenth-story window.

After conducting these experiments for over a decade, the CIA concluded that LSD was too unpredictable. One person might be given a dose of the drug and become silly and happy, while another, receiving the same dose, could experience frightening visions and completely lose touch with reality. LSD did not seem to be very useful as a truth drug or as a brainwashing tool either, and the projects were eventually shut down.

Ken Kesey, Timothy Leary, and the Hippie Counterculture

In 1959, one person taking part in these hallucinogenic drug studies was Ken Kesey, a creative writing student at

Stanford University. Kesey thought the drugs were fascinating, and he wondered how the experience would be different if he took them at home where he was comfortable, rather than at the VA hospital where the study was being conducted. He began sneaking the drugs out— LSD, psilocybin, mescaline, and others—and taking them back to share with his friends. The parties Kesey and his friends held with psychedelic drugs and effects like black lights and florescent paint contributed to the rising popularity of hallucinogenic drugs in the emerging hippie counterculture. The hippie counterculture was a rebellion against the traditional culture and ways of life, and drugs were often a part of this rebellion.

While Kesey and his friends spread the popularity of hallucinogenic drugs on the West Coast, in the East, hallucinogens were becoming better known as well. On June 10, 1957, *Life* magazine published an article called "Seeking the Magic Mushroom," by a New York City banker named R. Gordon Wasson. The article described how Wasson had traveled to a remote Indian village in Mexico and taken part in a sacred mushroom ritual, using hallucinogenic mushrooms. This article was the first many people had heard about hallucinogens.

In the summer of 1960, Timothy Leary, a psychology lecturer at Harvard University, traveled to Mexico himself to try the psilocybin mushrooms. He returned to Harvard feeling as though his life had been changed by his hallucinogenic experience, that he now saw the world differently, and that the drug had helped him discover "the god within." With a colleague, Richard Alpert, Leary began the Harvard Psychedelic Drug Research Program, a series of experiments studying the effects of psilocybin and other hallucinogens on people. One

Author Ken Kesey helped contribute to hallucinogens' popularity during the 1960s.

In the 1960s, Timothy Leary and Richard Alpert were two young professors at Harvard. Their names would become forever linked with LSD.

example of the project's work was the Concord Prison Experiment, a study on whether psilocybin could help keep prisoners from going back to a criminal lifestyle once they had been released. Leary believed the results of the experiment were promising, although in the long term the prisoners involved in the study reoffended at about the same rate as those who had never been given psilocybin.

Another study done by the research program was the Marsh Chapel Experiment in which twenty Harvard Divinity students were given either a dose of psilocybin or a *placebo*. The goal of the experiment was to see whether psilocybin would act as an entheogen—a drug that produces a spiritual experience—for those who were already spiritually minded. Those who received the psilocybin during the experiment believed that they had indeed had a mystical experience. Leary took this as further proof that hallucinogens actually did help people access deeper levels of consciousness.

In 1963, Leary and Alpert were both fired from Harvard, after university officials discovered they were giving LSD to undergraduate students. Leary moved to an estate outside of New York City and continued his research on psychedelic drugs. He also continued arguing for the usefulness of psychedelics in helping people expand their consciousness; he used the phrase "Turn on, tune in, drop out." People curious about LSD and other hallucinogens came from all over to meet Leary and to take drugs with him. At this point, most hallucinogens were still legal in the United States.

In 1964, Ken Kesey and a group of friends made a cross-country trip in an old school bus they painted and named *Further* (or later, *Furthur*). They called themselves

Ken Kesey and his friends the Merry Pranksters traveled across America in a brightly painted school bus.

the Merry Pranksters, a name that fit their wildly out-rageous way of living. When they reached New York, they dropped in to visit Timothy Leary, thinking their common interest in psychedelic drugs meant they would be kindred spirits. In reality, while both Leary and the Pranksters believed in the mind-expanding properties of hallucinogens, Leary's calm and intellectual way of ex-periencing a drug trip clashed with the Pranksters' laid-back attitude. For example, Leary believed the best way to take psychedelics was quietly and comfortably, with no distractions, while Kesey and Pranksters danced and partied with black lights and Day-Glo paint.

Not long after the first bus trip, Kesey and the Prank-sters began holding Acid Tests. This involved hundreds, sometimes thousands, of people all taking LSD together, while lights, colors, and music swirled around them. Part of the test was to see whether you could survive the

College students were influenced by the teachings of Leary and Kesey, creating a new subculture where LSD use was a part of a philosophy of love, free sex, and peace.

Peace signs, marijuana, and magic mushrooms all became symbols of the sixties' culture.

night, although it was also an attempt to get a large number of people to "expand their consciousness" at the same time.

Both Kesey and Leary influenced the growing drug culture of the 1960s. While young drug users were drawn to the carefree rebellion of the Merry Pranksters, the fact that Leary had been a respected Harvard professor let many people argue there was nothing harmful about hallucinogenic drugs. For this reason, President Richard Nixon once called Leary the most dangerous man in America.

Raves, Parties, and Club Drugs

On October 6, 1966, LSD became illegal in California, and the next year was banned throughout the United States. As a result, the drug became much more difficult to get. In 1970, the Controlled Substances Act banned most hallucinogenic drugs.

With hallucinogenic drugs now illegal and more difficult to find, and with young members of the hippie community growing up and joining the mainstream world, psychedelic drug use became less public. During the 1980s, LSD use decreased, although there was a small surge of PCP users in the late 1970s and early 1980s.

In the late 1990s, a type of party known as a rave began to become popular in the United States. Raves had been common in the United Kingdom and Europe a decade earlier. A rave is an all-night dance party, often held in an empty warehouse or other large out-of-the-way building. Common characteristics of the rave are electronic dance music, a dark or nearly dark building, dancing with glow sticks or LEDs, and, often, drugs.

How Many People Use Hallucinogens?

The group Monitoring the Future studies drug use among teenagers. In 2006, they recorded that

3.4 % of 8th graders,
6.1 % of 10th graders, and
8.3 % of 12th graders

had ever tried hallucinogens. Also,

0.9 % of 8th graders,
1.5 % of 10th graders, and
1.5 % of 12th graders

had used some kind of hallucinogenic drug in the thirty days prior to the survey.

Ecstasy became common at raves and parties, and ketamine was frequently used as well. Although ecstasy is not strictly a hallucinogen, it changes the way users perceive the world and can cause mild visual hallucinations at high doses. While the popularity of raves dropped in the 2000s, club drugs such as ecstasy continued to be used frequently.

So Why do People Use Hallucinogenic Drugs?

People take drugs for many reasons, but those who use hallucinogens can generally be divided into three groups.

Members of the Native American Church

While the United States has banned almost all hallucinogenic drugs, one major exception is peyote used in

Raves take place in nearly dark buildings enhanced with colored lights—and often hallucinogens.

American Indians who are members of the Native American Church use peyote in their traditional religious ceremonies.

The Native American Church merges traditional Native beliefs with Christian teachings, including a belief in angels. According to the church's teachings, Jesus Christ is revealed through peyote.

traditional Native American religious ceremonies. Only members of the Native American Church may use peyote, and then only in traditional religious ceremonies. Anyone may not become a member of the Native American Church; the only people eligible for membership are Native Americans who are part of a federally recognized tribe.

Researchers continue to explore whether LSD's mind-blowing effects might have beneficial uses in the fields of medicine or psychology.

People Looking for Legitimate Uses for Hallucinogens

Timothy Leary has not been the only person promoting the benefits of psychedelic drugs. A number of researchers, today and throughout the twentieth century, have studied hallucinogens, looking for possible uses for these drugs. Some look for medical uses, others for cultural ones—such as Leary's experiments with prisoners that looked at whether a hallucinogenic experience would help keep inmates from committing more crimes once they had been released.

Sometimes people experiment with hallucinogens because they hope they will have a mind-expanding and

Even people who do not belong to the Native American Church may use hallucinogens because they believe it will expand their souls, allowing them to perceive and connect with the spiritual world.

Hallucinogens—Unreal Visions 61

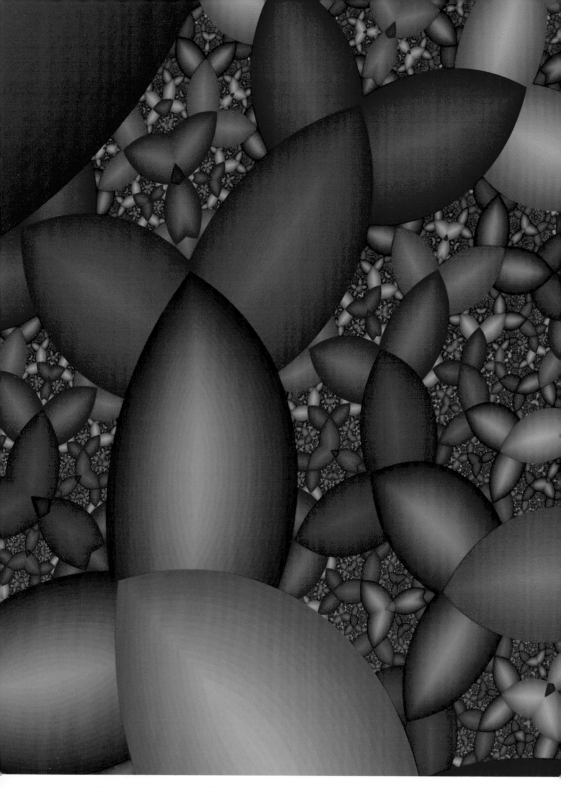

Many people who use LSD or other hallucinogens do so simply because they enjoy the bright colors and other bizarre perceptions.

life-changing experience. Some see these drugs as a way to connect with the spiritual world or with God. After taking a drug like LSD, some people do claim to have had such an experience; at least as often, however, a user has a negative experience, with *paranoia* and terrifying hallucinations. There is no way to predict which experience a person will have.

People Looking for a Good Time

Many young hallucinogen-users are not trying to find something religious or mind-expanding; they just want to have fun and they think taking hallucinogens might be interesting. Unfortunately for them, very real dangers are associated with hallucinogen use, and too many people discover the hard way there are better ways to have fun.

3 The Dangers of Hallucinogens

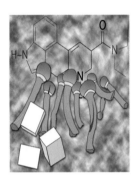

Everything Jesse looked at had grown rainbow-edged, dancing with swirling fractal patterns. Lisa smelled colors and tasted sounds, her senses mixing and blending. Meghan, curled in the corner, thought something was watching her, something terrifying trying to find a way into her room. Ryan felt a deep sense of connection with the world, as though the universe was communicating with him. Alex watched in horror as the posters on his wall turned monster-faced and fixed their burning eyes on him. Dayna, exhausted, feared she would never be normal again. Tony loved everyone—until they irritated him; then he hated them.

Seven people, seven different reactions to a hallucinogenic drug. The effects of hallucinogens can be extremely hard to predict; even if a person has taken the drug many times before they still might have a completely different experience the next time.

Not knowing what to expect is only one of the problems hallucinogenic drug users face. Hallucinogens can, in fact, be extremely dangerous in many ways.

Overdosing

Unlike many of the other illegal drugs, fatal overdoses of hallucinogens are extremely rare. While it is technically possible to overdose on LSD, for example, the amount needed would be thousands of times greater than a typical dose. For PCP, the amount would be a little less, but still many times higher than the average dose.

More dangerous than an overdose is the risk of a "bad trip," when a person experiences scary or unpleasant images or sensations while on a hallucinogen. The higher the dose and the more often a person takes a hallucinogen, the more likely he is to have a bad experience. Often, a bad trip is so terrifying and disagreeable that a person will avoid that drug, or all drugs, for fear of repeating the experience. Part of the problem with hallucinogens is that there is no way to know what dose level will produce a "bad trip." What seems to be a tiny amount of the drug may in fact contain such concetrated amounts of the chemical that it produces powerful effects.

Unknown Drugs

One very common problem drug users face is knowing what they are taking. Sometimes this is because someone has slipped something into a drink when a person was not paying attention. In this case, the person is not aware that she has taken any drug at all and she is completely unprepared when she starts becoming high.

Some people think it is funny to watch how a person acts when he begins hallucinating and acting strangely. In fact, it can be very dangerous; hallucinogenic drugs can cause people to put themselves and others in danger because, for example, they might believe they can jump off a roof and not be hurt or they

Each person's "trip" is unique; one may perceive distorted images, another may feel that time has slowed down, and yet another may be filled with strong emotions.

Ketamine is often referred to as the "date-rape drug" because it has been used by men wanting to take sexual advantage of a woman's drugged state.

might attack friends because they believe people are threatening them. This effect is even more extreme when the person does not know he has taken drugs and therefore does not realize what he is experiencing is caused by drugs.

Other drugs, such as ketamine and certain non-hallucinogens, can be used as date-rape drugs, which is another reason people should be careful of what they drink at parties. In the case of ketamine, the user becomes disoriented and begins to hallucinate, losing touch with her body and her own identity. A person can find it difficult to move. When the effects wear off, a person sometimes does not remember what happened while under the influence of the ketamine.

Even if a person knows he is taking drugs, he still may not know exactly what he is taking. Many drugs are contaminated with other drugs and chemicals, and this could cause unexpected effects. This contamination might be accidental, created when a drug was manufactured or packaged in a dirty place, or on the other hand, the drug could be a completely different substance from what the user expected. Sometimes drug dealers substitute something cheaper to save themselves money—at times this could be harmless and at others deadly. PCP is one of the cheaper drugs to manufacture and is frequently used as a substitute drug on the street.

Hallucinogenic plants and mushrooms can also be difficult to identify. Mushrooms can be tricky to identify, even for experienced people, and young people looking

Not all mushrooms are hallucinogenic and many are poisonous. Experimenting with them as a means to get high is very dangerous.

Toad Licking

A rumor has occasionally circulated saying that a person can get a hallucinogenic high by licking the backs of Cane Toads or Colorado River Toads, related species containing psychoactive chemicals in their skin and venom. In reality, these toads are also extremely poisonous and licking them could lead to severe illness or death.

Colorado River toads have psychoactive chemicals on their skin; licking them, however, can cause serious illness or death.

for a hallucinogenic experience have picked poisonous mushrooms that looked similar to the psychedelic fungi they were trying to find.

While identification mistakes can be a serious problem, the problem can be just as bad when people do find what they are looking for but do not understand the risks. For example, someone may find a plant he has heard is hallucinogenic, but not realize the same plant is also very poisonous. Belladonna, also called deadly nightshade, is a plant like this: while belladonna can cause powerful hallucinations, a very small amount can be fatal.

Jimson weed, from the same family as belladonna, is also occasionally eaten by teenagers looking for a cheap hallucinogen. According to the American Association of Poison Control Centers, in 1998, 152 cases of jimson weed poisoning were reported throughout the United States. This number includes only those cases in which someone called a Poison Control Center, so the number is probably actually higher. Without medical treatment, jimson weed poisoning can sometimes be fatal. Besides causing hallucinations, jimson weed can make a person jumpy and anxious, and cause seizures, coma, and amnesia. The effects might take days to wear off completely.

Combining Drugs

Many times, a person who uses hallucinogenic drugs will not take the hallucinogen by itself, but will also take another type of drug, such as marijuana. Often the person is in a place—like a party—where different kinds of drugs are being passed around. While the effects of a drug like LSD are very unpredictable at the best of times, combining it with other drugs makes the effects even more uncertain. Some drugs might cancel each other out, but

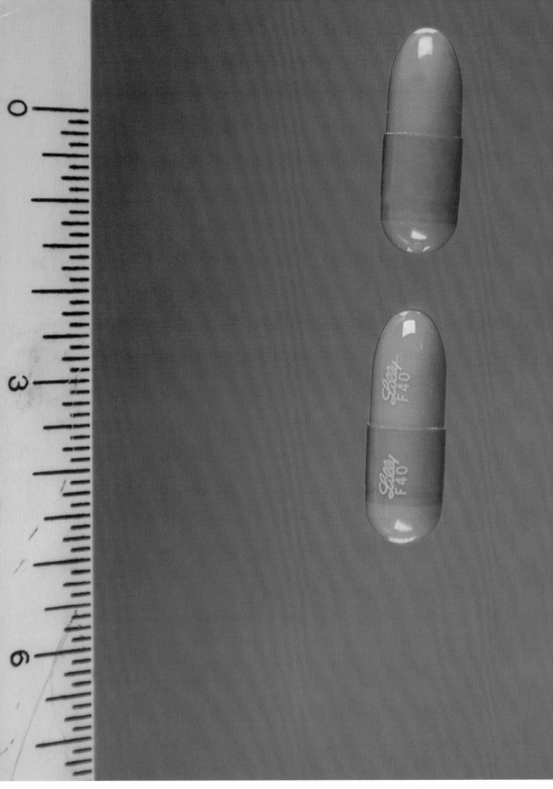

Using LSD at the same time a person is taking an antidepressant, such as Seconal, shown here, can be extremely dangerous.

more often the chemicals in the drugs combine to create a stronger, or very different, experience. Sometimes, teenagers at a party might have access to alcohol, cigarettes, marijuana, and other drugs such as hallucinogens. Taking these alone is harmful enough, but mixing even two could be deadly. The more drugs a person takes at the same time, the greater the chance the chemicals will interact to create dangerous effects.

Even legal drugs can interact with hallucinogens to cause problems. Taking LSD while on certain antidepressants has been known to cause seizures and death, and even caffeine, a stimulant, could increase the risk of agitation and paranoia while taking a hallucinogen. The chemicals in a person's brain exist in a delicate balance; putting dangerous substances like hallucinogens into your body throws off this balance. While the body is often able to process the chemicals with time and get rid of them, the more drugs and combinations of drugs, the more difficult it is for your body to remove the chemicals before they do serious damage.

How a Person Acts on Drugs

When a person takes hallucinogens, the way he sees the world around him changes. At times this leads a person to do things he would never have done if he had not been on the drug. One of the most common mistakes people make while under the influence of drugs or alcohol is deciding to have a sexual encounter. Drugs make it impossible to think clearly and make informed decisions; many people regret what they have done when the effect of the drug wears off. When people have sex while on hallucinogenic drugs, they are less likely to remember to use protection that would lessen the risk of sexually transmitted diseases and pregnancy. Decisions about sex should only be made completely sober and with a lot of thought.

Drugs like PCP, which act as dissociatives, can be especially dangerous. PCP is the strongest of these drugs, but ketamine and dextromethorphan (found in cough suppressants) are also dissociatives. When a person takes PCP she becomes dissociated—or out of touch—with the world and her own body. The drug causes the user to feel invincible, as though she could do anything and not get hurt. Added to this is the fact that PCP makes people much less sensitive to pain. Even though a person may really be getting hurt, she may not realize it at the time. Many horror stories are told of people committing violent murders or mutilating themselves while under the influence of PCP. Some of these stories have been exaggerated or made up to scare people out of doing drugs, but this does not mean PCP is harmless. In fact, any violent emotions a person has when she takes the drug are amplified and intensified. So if someone really did feel murderously angry before she took PCP, she might be led to actually commit violence.

Permanent Damage

Hallucinogens are sometimes called psychotomimetics. This means they make a person act as though he had a mental illness. When someone actually does have a mental illness, taking hallucinogens can destabilize his personality and cause a breakdown. Even if a person has not been diagnosed with a mental illness, hallucinogens can sometimes trigger a psychological breakdown in people who have a predisposition to such problems. While some people could guess that they might be predisposed to psychological problems, since, for example, other members of the family have been diagnosed with a psychiatric illness, others might have no warning that they were at risk until it is too late.

PCP in foil wrappers; this drug intensifies users' emotions.

LSD trips can be terrifying experiences that mimic schizophrenia.

An example is that of Frank Olson, the U.S. army biochemist who was slipped LSD during secret CIA testing of the drug. Olson, who had never before experienced psychological problems, fell apart completely. Long after the drugs had worn off, Olson remained paranoid, depressed, and agitated. Just before he was to be committed to a mental institution, he apparently threw himself out of his hotel room window.

The problems do not need to be as extreme as a total psychotic break; sometimes, if a person has a tendency to depression, hallucinogenic drugs can make the depression worse.

Flashbacks

One danger that occurs to many people when they think of hallucinogens, and especially LSD, is flashbacks. Stories have circulated that a person may take LSD once or twice when he was young and then, years later, suddenly have a hallucinogenic experience for no apparent reason. While this can be the case, the risks of flashbacks are much greater if a person has been a heavy LSD user, has had one or several bad trips, or has recently taken LSD. About a quarter of LSD users have reported experiencing flashbacks. Almost always, these flashbacks involve visual hallucinations, sometimes mild, such as halos of color around objects, sparkling trails of light, or seeing movement out the corner of the eye when nothing is there.

At one time, some people tried to explain flashbacks by claiming that LSD stayed in the body for years. The story said that crystals of LSD collected in the spinal fluid, occasionally being released into the blood and causing a hallucinogenic high, which was known as a flashback. The rumor was completely false, though. LSD is totally metabolized by the body in several days at most.

Scientists do not completely understand why flashbacks happen, but they have some ideas. One idea is that flashbacks are simply a memory of the hallucinogenic experience, similar to how memories from the past pass through a person's thoughts at apparently random times. As memories are often triggered by smells or other sensations, flashbacks can also be triggered by things such as using other drugs like marijuana or alcohol or by being very tired. Someone who has had a very bad experience using LSD can have a flashback similar to people with post-traumatic stress disorder who relive terrifying events long after they have happened.

Another idea is that LSD changes the way the brain sees things. Some researchers believe that using LSD makes permanent changes to the brain, teaching it to see things in a different way. When a flashback happens, this is because the brain is exercising what it has learned.

An extreme form of flashbacks is called hallucinogen-persisting perception disorder (HPPD). A person suffering from HPPD has trouble living a normal life because of her flashbacks. Sometimes the flashbacks last for only a minute or two and happen occasionally, but some people live with almost constant visual hallucinations. There is no treatment for HPPD, although some antidepressants can help. People with HPPD need to stop taking all drugs, however, since they usually make the disorder worse. Often, HPPD ends on its own, either gradually or suddenly, after months or years.

The dangers involved in taking hallucinogens are varied and there is no way a person could protect himself from

Some people who take LSD may experience recurring, frightening flashbacks.

Individuals who take hallucinogens may encounter a variety of psychiatric dangers; there is no way to predict who will experiences these symptoms and who will not.

all of them. This is especially true because of the unpredictable effects of hallucinogens.

One other major danger people who use hallucinogenic drugs face is that of legal consequences if they are caught. Drug convictions can change a person's life forever, ruining his plans for the future and sending his life in unwanted directions.

 Legal Consequences of Using Hallucinogens

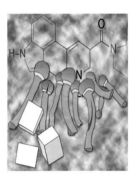

On November 25, 2003, William Leonard Pickard was sentenced to life in prison without parole for manufacturing LSD. His partner, Clyde Apperson, was sentenced to thirty years without parole. Three years earlier, DEA (Drug Enforcement Agency) agents had raided a site in Kansas and discovered Pickard and Apperson's laboratory in an old missile silo. This was the pair's third lab the DEA had raided in less than five years. In one of these labs, Pickard and Apperson made 2.2 pounds (1 kilogram) of LSD every five weeks—equal to ten million doses. The DEA had long suspected Pickard and Apperson were responsible for the majority of LSD in the United States; after their arrests, arrests involving LSD dropped by 95 percent.

Ever since the late 1960s, when President Richard Nixon declared a "war on drugs," the legal consequences for using drugs, selling them, or manufacturing or growing them have been harsh. With the increased popularity and availability of drugs during the 1960s, the entire world began to realize how dangerous they were. In 1971, the United Nations Convention on Psychotropic Substances went into effect, requiring countries that had signed the convention to ban all psychotropic—mind-altering—drugs except when used medically. Today, most countries have laws banning the use and sale of drugs such as hallucinogens.

In 1970, the United States passed the Controlled Substances Act. The Act divided drugs into groups, called schedules. Schedule I drugs have the most restrictions and the strictest penalties associated with them. They are described as drugs with no accepted medical uses and a high risk for abuse. Most hallucinogens are Schedule I drugs. PCP, originally used as an anesthetic, is classified as a Schedule II drug, and ketamine, which is still occasionally used as a veterinarian anesthetic, is classified as a Schedule III drug.

Crimes Related to Drugs

The most basic drug-related crime is possession. This means a person has an illegal drug with him, whether or not he intends to use the drug himself, sell it, or give it to a friend. If a person has a large amount of drugs with him, he may be charged with possession with intent to distribute, a more serious offense; laws usually declare that anything over a certain amount—an amount which varies from drug to drug, as well as from state to state—is more than anyone would reasonably have for personal use.

Controlled Substances Act

Schedule I

A. The drug or other substance has a high potential for abuse.
B. The drug or other substance has no currently accepted medical use in treatment in the United States.
C. There is a lack of accepted safety for use of the drug or other substance under medical supervision.

Schedule II

A. The drug or other substance has a high potential for abuse.
B. The drug or other substance has a currently accepted medical use in treatment in the United States or a currently accepted medical use with severe restrictions.
C. Abuse of the drug or other substances may lead to severe psychological or physical dependence.

Schedule III

A. The drug or other substance has a potential for abuse less than the drugs or other substances in schedules I and II.
B. The drug or other substance has a currently accepted medical use in treatment in the United States.
C. Abuse of the drug or other substance may lead to moderate or low physical dependence or high psychological dependence.

Schedule IV

A. The drug or other substance has a low potential for abuse relative to the drugs or other substances in schedule III.
B. The drug or other substance has a currently accepted medical use in treatment in the United States.
C. Abuse of the drug or other substance may lead to limited physical dependence or psychological dependence relative to the drugs or other substances in schedule III.

Schedule V

A. The drug or other substance has a low potential for abuse relative to the drugs or other substances in schedule IV.
B. The drug or other substance has a currently accepted medical use in treatment in the United States.
C. Abuse of the drug or other substance may lead to limited physical dependence or psychological dependence relative to the drugs or other substances in schedule IV.

Selling or distributing drugs is sometimes called drug trafficking. This can mean dealing in drugs on a very large scale, such as drug cartels that smuggle drugs across international lines, or it can mean smaller operations involving only a single dealer. Even if the amount of the drug is very small, a person can still be charged with trafficking if a police officer sees her give some to another person. Therefore, someone does not even need to sell drugs to be charged with trafficking—giving the drugs to a friend to hold for a moment would still be looked at as trafficking.

Another crime often associated with drugs is conspiracy. Conspiracy means that two or more people have agreed together to commit a crime. Someone can be charged with conspiracy if, for example, he lends his car to his brother who then uses the car to pick up a shipment of illegal drugs. Being friends with people who use and distribute drugs can be very dangerous, since apparently innocent actions could result in an arrest on conspiracy charges.

Sometimes, while using or distributing drugs, a person commits another crime. For example, a drug dealer may kill a rival. Another example would be a person who breaks into a house or commits a murder while under the influence of drugs, because the drug has lowered his inhibitions or strengthened violent emotions he already had. Hallucinogenic drugs, however, are less likely to influence a person to commit a violent crime than are certain other drugs, such as methamphetamine.

A special case of this type of crime is driving while under the influence of drugs. This is called DUI, or, sometimes DWI (Driving While Impaired) or OWI (Operating While Impaired). The exact term depends on

Driving while impaired is a crime; penalties become even stiffer if someone is injured or killed as a result.

If police discover that a person is driving LSD to another state to sell, the officer can impound the car.

88 Chapter 4—The Legal Dangers of Using Hallucinogens

the state where the crime was committed. If someone is injured or killed by a person who has been taking drugs or alcohol while driving, the penalties are much higher.

Drug Laws in the United States

The laws about illegal drugs can be very complicated. There are federal laws and state laws, and which law enforcement agency has jurisdiction depends on a number of factors. For example, a federal crime occurs whenever someone takes illegal drugs across a state line or takes them onto federal land, but there are other reasons as well.

The DEA, Drug Enforcement Agency, is a federal law enforcement agency whose responsibility is making sure the laws set out in the Controlled Substances Act are upheld. The federal minimum sentence for possession of 1 gram of LSD is five years and ten years for 10 grams. For PCP, possession of 10 grams gives a minimum sentence of five years, with a minimum of ten years for 100 grams. If someone is killed or seriously injured because a person has used LSD or PCP, the minimum sentence is doubled. The second offense of such a crime means a mandatory life sentence. Often, fines as large as several million dollars can go along with the prison term. Even a very small amount of drugs can completely change a person's life forever.

Federal laws also include forfeiture laws, meaning that federal agents can confiscate any property involved in a crime. For instance, if a person is using her car to drive to another state and sell LSD, law enforcement can take the car since it was used to commit the crime of drug trafficking. They can also take the person's house and belongings, since they were bought using the money from illegal drug sales. The purpose of these laws is to punish people involved in criminal activities and to use their assets to pay for crime prevention.

Forfeiture laws also involve property not actually owned by the person committing the crime. This means that if someone was, for example, collecting psilocybin mushrooms in the basement of his parents' home and drying them there to sell later, his parents could lose their home when he was arrested, if law enforcement agents have reason to believe they knew about their son's operation and did nothing to stop it.

While the Controlled Substances Act is the set of laws governing federal drug offenses, each state also has its own set of drug laws. In some states, possession of small amounts of certain drugs are classified as misdemeanors, lesser offenses that are generally punished with fines, **probation**, community service, or light prison sentences. Other states have tougher laws and almost all drug-related charges are felonies. Felonies have harsher penalties than misdemeanors and people also view them much more seriously. People with felony convictions on their records can find it difficult to find jobs, rent apartments, or be accepted to college (especially law school). They usually cannot own a gun or run for public office, and a few states permanently ban those who have been convicted of a felony from ever voting again.

Drug Laws in Canada

In Canada, the Controlled Drugs and Substances Act (CDSA) contains the laws concerning illegal drugs. Like the U.S. Controlled Substances Act, the CDSA also puts restricted drugs into schedules, although the Canadian and American drug schedules do not correspond with each other. The CDSA lays out eight drug schedules, and the schedule a person is charged under determines the maximum sentence he can receive. The strictest penalties are for offensives related to Schedule I drugs. The maximum penalty for possession of a Schedule I drug is seven years in prison and the maximum penalty for trafficking or producing a Schedule I drug is a life sentence.

In Canada, unlike in the United States, PCP and ketamine are placed on a higher schedule than LSD, psilocybin, and mescaline. PCP and ketamine are Schedule

An X-ray of a car allows DEA officers to see a hidden cache of drugs.

Teens who use illegal drugs can face severe legal penalties.

I drugs, subject to the maximum penalties, while LSD, psilocybin, and mescaline are Schedule III drugs. The penalties for Schedule III drugs include a maximum of three years in prison for possession and a maximum of ten years for trafficking or production. Peyote—from which mescaline is derived—is specifically excluded from the list of scheduled drugs.

Drugs and Teens

Some teens think they are safe when they experiment with drugs. Typically, the penalties for juvenile offenders are much lighter than for adults, and a person can petition the courts to have her record erased after she turns eighteen. Over the past decade, however, many of the laws protecting juvenile offenders have changed. Today, young offenders have less privacy than in the past, and their record can often continue to haunt them throughout their lives.

Bringing drugs onto school grounds can also create huge problems for students. Many schools have very strict policies about drugs on school property, and a student who breaks the rules can be suspended or even expelled. Losing even part of a school year can be difficult to catch up.

Laws in the United States have created Drug Free School Zones around schools, parks, and public housing. The purpose of the zones is to keep drug dealers away from kids and teens. Under the current laws, the zones extend 1,000 feet from school property and 500 feet from parks and public housing. Within the zones, penalties for drug convictions are greater, and the zones are usually patrolled more attentively. In 2006, some lawmakers began

Many schools have drug-free zones that are intended to keep students safe from drug dealers.

asking for smaller zones but with increased penalties for convictions. Many cities have so many Drug Free School Zones that the zones overlap and cover almost the entire city. This means, basically, that the city has simply toughened their drug laws and the original intent of the law—to keep drugs away from kids—is lost.

Legal consequences of using drugs, or of simply holding them for a friend, can be extremely serious. Law enforcement agencies have spent billions of dollars working to wipe out illegal drug use—patrolling the streets, arresting and imprisoning dealers, and educating the public about the dangers of drugs.

Some people believe too much money has been spent fighting the war on drugs, and possibly, they argue, these drugs could have legitimate uses.

5 Controversial Issues

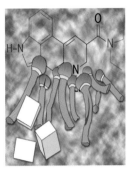

Talking about hallucinogenic drugs brings out strong feelings in some people. Clearly, law enforcement agencies such as the DEA and health related organizations such as the National Institute on Drug Abuse (NIDA) believe hallucinogens are dangerous drugs that need to be kept illegal. Former NIDA director Alan Leshner wrote in a research report that

> These drugs [hallucinogens and dissociatives] can disrupt a person's ability to think and communicate rationally, or even to recognize reality, sometimes resulting in bizarre or dangerous behavior. Hallucinogens such as LSD cause emotions to swing wildly and real-world sensations to assume unreal, sometimes frightening aspects. Dissociative drugs like PCP and ketamine may make a user feel disconnected and out of control.

On the other hand, some people think hallucinogens like LSD should be made legal, or at least allowed for medical use. Albert Hofmann, creator of LSD, wrote, "I see the true importance of LSD in the possibility of providing material aid to meditation aimed at the mystical experience of a deeper, comprehensive reality. Such a use accords entirely with the essence and working character of LSD as a sacred drug." John Horgan, a science journalist, wrote in an article for *Slate*, "Adults seeking solace or insight ought to be allowed to consume psychedelics such as LSD, psilocybin, and mescaline."

The Legalization Debate

Ever since the War on Drugs took off in the 1970s, Americans have argued about whether it helped or hurt the country. Even people who believe drugs are harmful don't all agree with the actions taken by the War on Drugs.

Mescaline, a hallucinogenic substance, is derived from the peyote cactus.

Dr. Benson Roe, a retired heart surgeon who campaigns for the legalization of drugs, believes that making drugs legal would allow the FDA (Food and Drug Administration) to oversee the production and sale of these drugs. This would mean the FDA could make sure the drugs were not contaminated. If recreational drugs were legal, Roe argues, billions of dollars would be saved that is now being used on drug prevention, law enforcement, and keeping people in prison for drug-related crimes. Since most gangs earn their money through trafficking in illegal drugs and many homicides are drug-related, these problems would be greatly reduced by legalizing drugs.

In direct reaction to arguments like the ones made by Dr. Roe, the DEA has put together a booklet called, "Speaking out Against Drug Legalization." The DEA's reasons why drugs should not be legalized include:

- We have made significant progress in fighting drug use and drug trafficking in America. Now is not the time to abandon our efforts.
- Illegal drugs are illegal because they are harmful.
- Legalization of drugs will lead to increased use and increased levels of addiction.
- Crime, violence, and drug use go hand-in-hand.

Since hallucinogenic drugs are not usually as common as many other illegal drugs, the legalization debate is more often focused on drugs as an entire group or else on the legalization of marijuana. Some believe that hallucinogens like LSD and dissociatives like PCP are too powerful and too unpredictable for anyone to be able to use them safely. Others think hallucinogens are harmless if used responsibly, and that people should therefore be allowed the freedom to use them. A number of scientists and researchers,

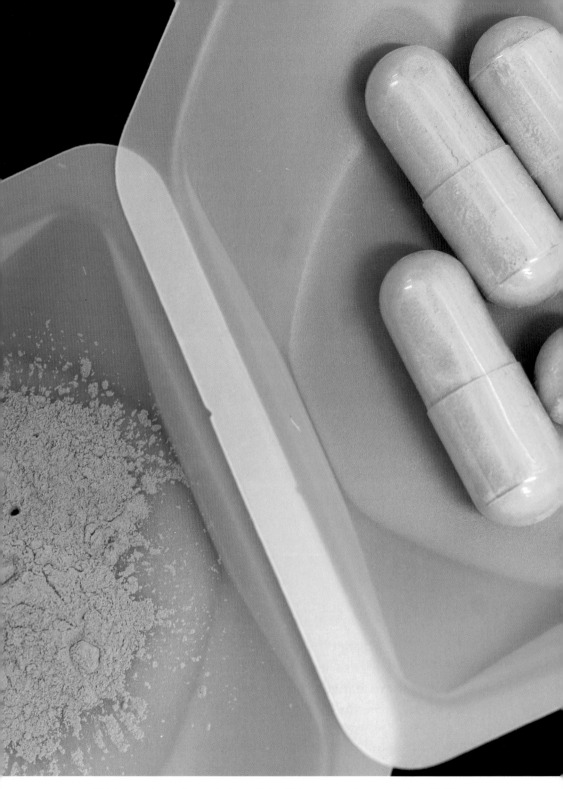

LSD in powder and capsule form; if the FDA oversaw the production of LSD, it could ensure that capsules like these contained uncontaminated drugs.

Hallucinogens like LSD or peyote could be effective treatments for alcoholism.

however, have argued for allowing hallucinogens to be studied to find legitimate uses for them. UCLA Professor of Public Policy Mark A. R. Kleiman wrote on his Web site in 2003 that "the claims for medical and religious use [of hallucinogenic drugs] are, in political terms, relatively plausible." One hallucinogen—peyote—is already legal in the United States when used in religious ceremonies by the Native American Church; so why shouldn't the same right be extended to other groups seeking to expand their spirituality through hallucinogens? In the 1990s, U.S. laws were changed to allow preapproved researchers to conduct experiments with Schedule I drugs like LSD and psilocybin using human test subjects. This has led to a number of studies on possible medical and therapeutic uses for hallucinogenic drugs.

Medical and Therapeutic Uses
for Hallucinogenic Drugs

Because hallucinogenic drugs have such a large effect on the way a person's mind works and how he experiences reality, many of the possible uses for hallucinogens researchers have suggested involve treatment for psychological disorders. For example, in the 1950s, before hallucinogens were banned, the drugs were sometimes used during *psychotherapy* sessions to help people better understand themselves and why they acted the way they did. Several studies in the 1960s also looked at using LSD as a treatment for children with *autism* and for childhood schizophrenia, with some apparent success.

Studies in the late 1950s using a single large dose of LSD as treatment for alcoholism showed success rates of about 50 percent. An article published in 1974 in the *American Journal of Psychiatry* described how peyote was a helpful part of treating alcoholism in Native Americans, when combined with other forms of therapy. In the 1990s, a company run by Howard Lotsof treated people

The Father of LSD Turns 100

Early in 2007, Albert Hofmann, who first discovered LSD, looked back on his life as he celebrated his hundredth birthday. He told the New York Times that he still considered LSD to be "medicine for the soul," and that he was frustrated by the worldwide prohibition that had pushed it underground. "It was used very successfully for 10 years in psychoanalysis," he said. He added that he felt that the youth movement of the 1960s had "hijacked" LSD, which had led to the rest of society demonizing it. Although he admitted that LSD is dangerous, he indicated that he felt that its misuse had led to its current reputation, which ignores the possible beneficial uses of his chemical child.

Albert Hofmann, the Father of LSD, turned 100 in 2007.

addicted to a variety of drugs using ibogaine, a mild hallucinogen. Because ibogaine is a Schedule I drug, Lotsof conducted his research in the Netherlands.

In December of 2006, the results of a preliminary study examining the possibility of using psilocybin to treat **obsessive-compulsive disorder** (OCD) were released. The study, conducted by Dr. Francisco Moreno of the University of Arizona, found that in all of the nine patients, psilocybin eliminated all the OCD symptoms in a matter of hours, leaving the patients symptom-free for several days. Since so few people were involved, however, not all scientists were impressed with Dr. Moreno's results.

Dr. Charles Grob of Harbor-UCLA Medical Center in Torrance, California, began a study in 2004, looking at the effect of psilocybin on the anxiety of dying cancer patients. Because of the strict requirements of the study—the patient needed to have end-stage terminal cancer but be otherwise healthy, and also needed to be interested in trying psilocybin to deal with her anxiety about death—Grob had some difficulty finding volunteers. However, as of the spring of 2006, six patients had participated in the study and appeared to have been helped by the treatment.

As of early 2007, Dr. John Halpern and Dr. Andrew Sewell of Harvard Medical School were in the process of seeking approval to do a study looking at whether LSD could help treat cluster headaches—a rare and extremely painful type of headaches that happen in clusters. Halpern and Sewell were first approached with the idea for the study by a group of cluster headache sufferers who had tried hallucinogens and found them helpful. These sufferers wanted a scientific study that could lead to hallucinogens eventually being accepted as a legitimate medical treatment for cluster headaches.

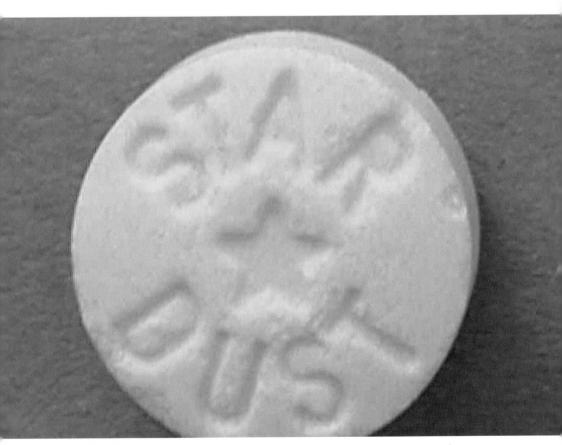

The FDA has approved a research study that examines the effectiveness of ecstasy as a treatment for post-traumatic stress syndrome.

Researchers are investigating whether LSD could be used to treat cluster headaches.

One Flew Over the Cuckoo's Nest

According to literary legend, Ken Kesey wrote much of his best-selling novel *One Flew Over the Cuckoo's Nest* while high on LSD. The novel was at the very least inspired by his early experiences with LSD in clinical trials. The book's plot deals with questions of authority versus rebellion, culture versus counterculture—and what's normal? who's insane?—the people society labels "insane" or the people in charge? Kesey believed that the perception-altering qualities of LSD (in contrast to the hallucinogenic qualities of mescaline and psilocybin) were useful tools for transcending rational consciousness and attaining a higher level of consciousness. This higher level of consciousness could then enhance a person's natural creativity.

Fractal art sometimes tries to reproduce the colors and sensations of a LSD trip.

Do Hallucinogens Make You More Creative?

Those who defend hallucinogenic drug use often describe how mind-expanding the experience has been, how the world began to make sense to them, to look beautiful and connected. Hallucinogens are known for causing people to see things that aren't there—things like rainbow edges and sparkles of light following moving objects. Sometimes people have more complete hallucinations as well, in which objects seem to be moving or shifting their shape and texture.

Because of these changes in perception, some artists claim hallucinogens increase their creativity. Psychedelic art and psychedelic music are types of art related to hallucinogenic drug experiences. Sometimes, psychedelic art and music are created while the artist is under the influence of a hallucinogen, or else these forms of art and music are attempts by the artist to recreate his experiences at a later time.

In the 1950s, psychiatrist Oscar Janiger conducted an experiment looking at the effects of LSD on creativity. Janiger took volunteers and had them draw or paint a picture of a Native American kachina doll before they took the LSD and then again an hour after taking it. The results showed dramatically different types of pictures when comparing the works created before and after taking LSD.

Since a person generally tries to recreate what he experiences, the product—whether art or music—would naturally be different when recreating a psychedelic experience. Also, since hallucinogens tend to lower inhibitions, psychedelic art tends to have bolder lines and brighter colors.

Kachina doll drawn before using LSD during Janiger's experiment.

Kachina doll drawn by same artist after using LSD.

Chapter 5—Controversial Issues

While hallucinogens certainly can affect the art and music someone produces, however, there is not much evidence that they make him more creative. For example, the best psychedelic art is done by those who are already artists. Hallucinogen users have occasionally produced what they believed was an artwork of great beauty and insight and woken up the next day to discover only meaningless smears of color. Simply taking hallucinogens does not give a person artistic talent, although a person may believe she has created great art while she is under the influence of the drug.

Using LSD may release a person's creativity—but it will not give her talent she does not already possess.

Overall, hallucinogenic drugs are complicated chemicals, causing varied and unpredictable results in those who use them. Because of the effects hallucinogens have on perceptions, people have often believed these drugs were showing them deeper meanings about the world or helping them connect with gods or their own unconscious minds. Hallucinogens, however, can be extremely dangerous. While legitimate medical or therapeutic uses may be found for these drugs in the future, taking them with friends or alone could be extremely dangerous or even deadly.

Glossary

autism: A developmental disorder, which causes impaired communication, abnormal behavior, and emotional detachment.

catatonic: A state characterized by a complete lack of movement, activity, or expression.

metabolism: The processes within a body that break down introduced substances in order to provide energy or to remove harmful chemicals.

obsessive-compulsive disorder: A mental disorder that causes the need, or compulsion, to repeatedly complete tasks, such as handwashing, in order to deal with obsessive thoughts, such as worries about germs.

opiate: A drug containing opium, or one that mimics the effects of such a drug.

paranoia: A mental disorder, which causes the individual to suffer from irrational feelings of being watched or chased; also an extreme distrust of others for no logical reason.

placebo: A substance given to an individual who thinks it is a drug, when in reality it is a sugar-pill, or some other non-drug. Often used as a control in experimental drug trials.

probation: A trial period, during which an individual who has committed a crime is allowed to go free under the supervision of a probation officer.

psychoactive: Having an extreme effect on the mind, mood, or other mental processes.

psychotherapy: Treatment of mental disorders with psychological techniques that include talking about problems and their underlying causes so that solutions can be found.

schizophrenia: A severe mental disorder characterized by loss of touch with reality and a deterioration of thought patterns and behavior, which can include delusions or hallucinations.

sedative: A drug that has a calming, soothing, or tranquilizing effect on the user.

stimulant: A drug, such as caffeine, that causes increased activity, especially of the nervous or cardiovascular systems.

Further Reading

Barter, James. *Hallucinogens*. San Diego, Calif.: Lucent Books, 2002.

Furst, Peter E. *Mushrooms: Psychedelic Fungi*. Philadelphia: Chelsea House Publications, 2002.

Kuhn, Cynthia, Scott Swartzwelder, and Wilkie Wilson. *Buzzed: The Straight Facts about the Most Used and Abused Drugs, from Alcohol to Ecstasy*. New York: W. W. Norton & Company, 1998.

Littell, Mary Ann. *LSD*. Springfield, N.J.: Enslow Publishers, 1996.

Mehling, Randi. *Hallucinogens*. Philadelphia: Chelsea House Publications, 2003.

Newman, Gerald and Eleanor Newman Layfield. *PCP*. Springfield, N.J.: Enslow Publishers, 2000.

Olive, M. Foster. *Peyote and Mescaline*. Philadelphia: Chelsea House Publications, 2007.

Petechuk, David. *LSD*. San Diego, Calif.: Lucent Books, 2004.

Phillips, Jane Ellen. *LSD, PCP, & Other Hallucinogens*. Philadelphia: Chelsea House Publishers, 2000.

Schroeder, Brock E. *Ecstasy*. Philadelphia: Chelsea House Publishers, 2004.

Williams, Mary E., ed. *Hallucinogens*. Farmington Hills, Mich.: Greenhaven Press, 2005.

For More Information

Drug Enforcement Agency (DEA)
www.dea.gov

DEA Demand Reduction, Street Smart Prevention
www.justthinktwice.com

Monitoring the Future
www.monitoringthefuture.org

D.A.R.E. (Drug Abuse Resistance Education)
www.dare.com

National Institute on Drug Abuse (NIDA)
www.nida.nih.gov

Multidisciplinary Association for Psychedelic Studies (MAPS)
www.maps.org

The Web sites listed on this page were active at the time of publication. The publisher is not responsible for Web sites that have changed their addresses or discontinued operation since the date of publication. The publisher will review and update the Web-site list upon each reprint.

Bibliography

Albaugh, Bernard J. and Philip O. Anderson. "Peyote in the Treatment of Alcoholism Among American Indians." Nov. 1974. *The American Journal of Psychiatry*. http://ajp.psychiatryonline.org/cgi/content/abstract/131/11/1247.

"Arylcyclohexylamines: PCP and Ketamine." http://www.drugtext.org/sub/pcp1.html.

Barter, James. *Hallucinogens*. San Diego, Calif.: Lucent Books, 2002.

Bellenir, Karen, ed. *Drug Information for Teens: Health Tips about the Physical and Mental Effects of Substance Abuse*. Detroit, Mich.: Omnigraphics, 2002.

Bender, L. "Theory and Treatment of Childhood Schizophrenia." 1968. *Acta paedopsychiatrica*. On *neurodiversity.com*. http://www.neurodiversity.com/library_bender_1968.html.

Berger, Gilda. *Drug Abuse: The Impact on Society*. New York: Franklin Watts, 1988.

Brown University. "Other Drugs." *Health Information: Alcohol, Tobacco & Other Drugs*. http://www.brown.edu/Student_Services/Health_Services/Health_Education/atod/od_geninfo.htm.

Chan, Kit. "Jimson Weed Poisoning: A Case Report." *Complimentary and Alternative Medicine*. Fall 2002. The Permanente Journal. http://xnet.kp.org/permanentejournal/fall02/jimson.html.

Christman, Steve. "Datura stramonium." 9 Mar. 2004. *Floridata*. http://floridata.com/ref/d/datu_str.cfm.

CJOnline. "In-Depth: Kansas Missile Silos." *The Topeka Capital Journal*. 2007. http://www.cjonline.com/indepth/missilesilos/.

ClusterBusters. *Hallucinogenic Treatment of Neuro-Vascular Headaches*. http://www.clusterbusters.com/.

Clusterheadaches.com. http://www.clusterheadaches.com/.

Cockburn, Alexander and Jeffrey St. Clair. *Whiteout: The CIA, Drugs and the Press.* New York: Verso, 1998.

DEA: U.S. Drug Enforcement Administration. http://www.dea.gov/.

DEA (Drug Enforcement Administration). *Speaking Out Against Drug Legalization.* May 2003. http://www.usdoj.gov/dea/demand/ speakout/index.html.

DEA Demand Reduction: Street Smart Prevention. http://www.just-thinktwice.com/.

Dept. of English and American Studies, Vienna University, ed. "Tom Wolfe: The Electric Kool-Aid Acid Test." *Easy Riders: On the Road in American Culture.* 10 May 2002. http://www.univie.ac.at/ Anglistik/easyrider/data/tom_wolfe.htm.

De Rienzo, Paul and Dana Beal. *The Staten Island Project: The Ibogaine Story.* On *Cures Not Wars.* http://www.cures-not-wars.org/ibogaine/iboga.html.

Dodgson, Rick. *Merry Prankster History Project.* 27 May 2003. http:// www.prankstersweb.org/frontdoor.htm.

"Doubts spread about drug-free school zone laws." 23 March 2006. MSNBC. http://www.msnbc.msn.com/id/11964167/.

"Ecstasy approved for medical study." 25 Feb. 2004. CNN. http:// www.cnn.com/2004/HEALTH/02/25/ecstasy.study/index.html.

Ehrman, Mark. "The Heretical Dr. X." 2 Mar. 2003. *The Los Angeles Times.* On *Just Say Know.* http://www.just-say-know.com/articles/ misc/drx.txt.

Erowid: Documenting the Complex Relationship between Humans and Psychoactives. http://www.erowid.org/.

Ferrington, Adam J. "Psychotropic drug research receives approval from FDA." 2 Jan. 2005. *The Columbia Chronicle.* On *Washington Week.* http://www.pbs.org/weta/washingtonweek/voices/200501/ 0102nat1.html.

Fisher, Gary. "Treatment of Childhood Schizophrenia Utilizing LSD and Psilocybin." Summer 1997. *Newsletter of the Multidisci-*

plinary Association for Psychedelic Studies. On *The Albert Hofmann Foundation*. http://www.hofmann.org/papers/fisher/fisher_4.htm.

Frood, Arran. "Cluster busters." 28 Dec. 2006. *nature.com* On MAPS (*Multidisciplinary Association for Psychedelic Studies*). http://www.maps.org/sys/nq.pl?id=1147.

Grob, Charles S. *Psychiatric Research Study for Cancer Patients*. http://www.canceranxietystudy.org/.

Gwynne, Peter. *Who Uses Drugs?* New York: Chelsea House Publishers, 1988.

Hartman, Rich. "Medical Uses for Hallucinogens." *totse.com*. http://www.totse.com/en/drugs/psychedelics/med_lsd.html.

Hickman, Katy. "The Trip of a Lifetime." 5 April 2006. *BBC News*. http://news.bbc.co.uk/2/hi/uk_news/magazine/4877462.stm.

Hoffer, Abram. "Treatment of Alcoholism with Psychedelic Therapy." *Psychedelics: The Uses and Implications of Psychedelic Drugs*. Eds. Bernard Aaronson and Humphry Osmond. 1970. On *Shaffer Library of Drug Policy*. http://www.druglibrary.org/schaffer/lsd/hoffer.htm.

Hofmann, Albert. *LSD: My Problem Child*. 1980. http://www.flashback.se/archive/my_problem_child/.

Hofmann Foundation. *The Albert Hofmann Foundation*. http://www.hofmann.org/index.html.

Horgan, John. "Tripping De-Light Fantastic: Are Psychedelic Drugs Good for You?" 7 May 2003. *Slate*. http://www.slate.com/id/2082647/.

Hunter, Edward, consult. "Communist Psychological Warfare (Brainwashing)." 13 March 1958. *Committee on Un-American Activities, House of Representatives, Eighty-fifth Congress*. http://www.crossroad.to/Quotes/globalism/Congress.htm.

Hyde, Margaret O. and John F. Setaro. *Drugs 101: An Overview for Teens*. Brookfield, Conn.: Twenty-First Century Books, 2003.

Kleiman, Mark A. R. "*Slate* Lights the Trip Fantastic." [Weblog entry.] 7 May 2003. *Mark A. R. Kleiman: A Fair and Balanced Weblog*.

http://markarkleiman.blogspot.com/2003_05_01_markarkleiman_archive.html.

Kolb, Eli. *Eleusis: Alternative Addiction Treatment Program using Psychedelic Psychotherapy.* http://www.eleusis.us/.

Kuhn, Cynthia, Scott Swartzwelder, and Wilkie Wilson. *Buzzed: The Straight Facts about the Most Used and Abused Drugs, from Alcohol to Ecstasy.* New York: W. W. Norton & Company, 1998.

Kuhn, Cynthia and Wilkie Wilson. "Medicinal Muse." 9 Aug. 2000. *Salon.com.* http://archive.salon.com/health/addiction/drugs/2000/08/09/creativity/index.html.

Kurtzweil, Paula. "Medical Possibilities for Psychedelic Drugs." Sept. 1995. *FDA Consumer Magazine.* http://www.fda.gov/FDAC/features/795_psyche.html.

Laurance, Jeremy. "LSD helps alcoholics put down the bottle." 6 Dec. 2006. *Belfast Telegraph.* http://www.belfasttelegraph.co.uk/incoming/article2047143.ece.

Lee, Martin A. and Bruce Schlain. "LSD and Creativity." *Acid Dreams: The Complete Social History of LSD: The CIA, the Sixties and Beyond.* 1985. http://www.levity.com/aciddreams/samples/creativity.html.

Leland, John. "Psychedelia's Middle-Aged Head Trip." 18 Nov. 2001. *The New York Times.* http://www.maps.org/media/nytimes11.18.01.html.

Lewis, Judith. "The Hallucinogenic Way of Dying." 18 Mar. 2004. *LA Weekly News.* http://www.laweekly.com/news/news/the-hallucinogenic-way-of-dying/1895/.

Littell, Mary Ann. *LSD.* Springfield, N.J.: Enslow Publishers, 1996.

MAPS (Multidisciplinary Association for Psychedelic Studies). *LSD and Psilocybin Research.* http://www.maps.org/research

MAPS (Multidisciplinary Association for Psychedelic Studies). *MDMA Research Information.* http://www.maps.org/mdma/.

MAPS (Multidisciplinary Association for Psychedelic Studies). *Psychedelic Research Around the World*. http://www.maps.org/research/index.html.

Moreno, Francisco A., Pedro Delgado, and Alan J. Gelenberg. *Effects of Psilocybin in Obsessive-Compulsive Disorder*. On MAPS (Multidisciplinary Association for Psychedelic Studies). http://www.maps.org/research/psilo/azproto.html.

Mulholland, Neil. "Use Your Illusions." Summer 2005. *Tate Etc*. http://www.tate.org.uk/tateetc/issue4/summeroflove2.htm.

Newman, Gerald and Eleanor Newman Layfield. *PCP*. Springfield, N.J.: Enslow Publishers, 1997.

NIDA (National Institute for Drug Abuse). "Mind over Matter: Hallucinogens." *NIDA for Teens: The Science Behind Drug Abuse*. http://teens.drugabuse.gov/mom/mom_hal1.asp.

OASAS. "Jimson Weed (Datura Stramonium)." *Drugs of Abuse*. New York State Office of Alcoholism and Substance Abuse Services (OASAS). http://www.oasas.state.ny.us/AdMed/drugs/FYI-Jimson.cfm.

Office of National Drug Control Policy (ONDCP). http://www.whitehousedrugpolicy.gov/.

Opar, Susan. *Hallucinogens and Creativity*. http://www.siena.edu/boswell/Drug%20Projects/Susan/drugs.htm.

Peterson, Robert C. and Richard C. Stillman, eds. *Phencyclidine (PCP) Abuse: An Appraisal*. Aug. 1978. NIDA Research Monograph 21. http://www.nida.nih.gov/pdf/monographs/21.pdf.

Philipkoski, Kristen. "Long Trip for Psychedelic Drugs." 27 Sept. 2004. *Wired News*. http://www.wired.com/news/medtech/0,1286,65025,00.html?tw=wn_story_mailer.

Phillips, Jane Ellen. *LSD, PCP, & Other Hallucinogens*. Philadelphia, Chelsea House Publishers, 2000.

"Pickard and Apperson Convicted of LSD Charges: Largest LSD Lab Seizure in DEA History." 31 March 2003. *U.S. Drug Enforcement Administration.* http://www.usdoj.gov/dea/pubs/states/newsrel/2003/sanfran033103.html.

Pooterland.com. "Through the Looking Glass: The Merry Prankster." 18 Aug. 2002. *Pooter's Psychedelic Shack.* http://www.pooterland.com/index2/looking_glass/merry_pranksters/merry_pranksters.html.

Pringle, Colin. "Ken Kesey and the Merry Pranksters." 6 Dec. 1995. *The Wild Bohemian.* http://wild-bohemian.com/kesey.htm.

Psych-Net-UK. "Hallucinogen Persisting Perception Disorder." 20 July 2003. *Disorder Information Sheets.* http://www.psychnet-uk.com/dsm_iv/hppd.htm.

R. C. "B.C.'s Acid Flashback." 8 Dec. 2001. *Vancouver Sun.* On *MAPS (Multidisciplinary Association for Psychedelic Studies).* http://www.maps.org/media/bcflashback.html.

Richardson, P. Mick. *Flowering Plants: Magic in Bloom.* New York: Chelsea House Publishers, 1986.

Rick, Matthew. *Tarnished Galahad: The Prose and Pranks of Ken Kesey.* http://www.ulster.net/~shady/thesis.html.

Roe, Benson B. "Why we should legalize drugs." *Schaffer Library of Drug Policy.* http://druglibrary.org/schaffer/Misc/roe1.htm.

Ross, Colin. "The CIA and Military Mind Control Research: Building the Manchurian Candidate." *CKLN-FM Mind Control Series—Part 1.* http://www.mindcontrolforums.com/radio/ckln01.htm.

Rumsey, Ken. "Ken Kesey." *The Beat Page.* http://www.rooknet.com/beatpage/writers/kesey.html.

Salak, John. *Drugs in Society: Are They our Suicide Pill?* New York: Twenty-First Century Books, 1993.

Salomone, Joseph A., III. "Toxicity, Hallucinogen." 12 Dec. 2006. *eMedicine.* http://www.emedicine.com/emerg/topic223.htm.

SAMHSA (Substance Abuse and Mental Health Services Administration). "Tips for Teens: The Truth About Hallucinogens." *National Clearinghouse for Alcohol and Drug Information.* http://ncadi.samhsa.gov/govpubs/PHD642/.

Sandberg, Nick. *Ibogaine.* http://www.ibogaine.co.uk/index.htm.

Schaffer, Amanda. "What a Long Strange Trip It's Been: Ecstasy, the New Prescription Drug?" 23 Jan. 2007. *Slate.* http://www.slate.com/id/2158144.

Scheindlin, Stanley. "A Brief History of Pharmacology." *Modern Drug Discovery.* May 2001. http://pubs.acs.org/subscribe/journals/mdd/v04/i05/html/05timeline.html.

Schroeder, Brock E. *Ecstasy.* Philadelphia: Chelsea House Publishers, 2004.

Simmons, James Q., III, Stanley J. Leiken, O. Ivar Lovaas, Benson Schaeffer, and Bernard Perloff. "Modification of Autistic Behavior with LSD-25." May 1966. *American Journal of Psychiatry.* On *neurodiversity.com.* http://www.neurodiversity.com/library_simmons_1966.html.

South Carolina Department of Alcohol and Other Drug Abuse Services. *Fact Sheet: PCP.* Sept. 2001. http://www.daodas.state.sc.us/documents/pcpfs.pdf.

Special Collections Department, University of Virginia Library. *The Psychedelic '60s: Literary Tradition and Social Change.* 28 Jan. 2004. http://www.lib.virginia.edu/small/exhibits/sixties/index.html.

Stafford, Peter. *Psychedelics Encyclopedia.* Berkeley, Calif.: Ronin Publishing, 1978.

Strassman, Rick J. "Hallucinogenic Drugs in Psychiatric Research and Treatment: Perspectives and Prospects." *The Journal of Nervous and Mental Disease.* 1995. On *Schaffer Library of Drug Policy.* http://www.druglibrary.org/schaffer/lsd/rjspap.htm.

"Study: Psilocybin Relieves OCD Symptoms." 21 Dec. 2006. CBS *News.* http://www.cbsnews.com/stories/2006/12/21/ap/health/main-D8M4TGR81.shtml.

Teen Drug Abuse. http://www.teendrugabuse.us/index.html.

Thomas, Gordon. *Journey into Madness: The True Story of Secret CIA Mind Control and Medical Abuse.* New York: Bantam Books, 1989.

"Toad Licking: The Latest High." totse.com. http://www.totse.com/en/drugs/rare_and_exotic_drugs/toadlick.html.

University of Alberta. "LSD treatment for alcoholism gets new look." [Weblog entry.] 6 Oct. 2006. *Science Blog.* http://www.scienceblog.com/cms/lsd-treatment-for-alcoholism-gets-new-look-11680.html.

University of Maryland. "Drug Information." 1 Feb. 2007. *Center for Substance Abuse Research (CESAR).* http://www.cesar.umd.edu/cesar/drug_info.asp.

University of Michigan. *Monitoring the Future.* 2006. http://monitoringthefuture.org/.

Williams, Mary E., ed. *Hallucinogens.* Farmington Hills, Mich.: Greenhaven Press, 2005.

Wolfe, Tom. *The Electric Kool-Aid Acid Test.* New York: Bantam Books, 1968.

Wong, George. "Ergot of Rye II: The Story of LSD." *Magical Mushrooms and Mystical Molds.* 2003. http://www.botany.hawaii.edu/faculty/wong/BOT135/Botany135syllabus(2003).htm.

Index

Picture Credits

Author and Consultant Biographies

Author

Sheila Nelson has written twenty-two educational books for young people. She lives in Rochester, New York, with her husband and two children.

Series Consultant

Jack E. Henningfield, Ph.D., is a professor at the Johns Hopkins University School of Medicine, and he is also Vice President for Research and Health Policy at Pinney Associates, a consulting firm in Bethesda, Maryland, that specializes in science policy and regulatory issues concerning public health, medications development, and behavior-focused disease management. Dr. Henningfield has contributed information relating to addiction to numerous reports of the U.S. Surgeon General, the National Academy of Sciences, and the World Health Organization.